Written by Christopher Nicholas
Illustrated by Greg Harris

**Reviewed by Frank Indiviglio, Zoologist, Wildlife Conservation Society, New York.**

Published by McClanahan Book Company, Inc.
A Division of Learning Horizons
1 American Road, Cleveland OH 44144
ISBN: 0-7681-0233-2
Printed in the U.S.A.
10 9 8 7 6 5 4 3 2 1

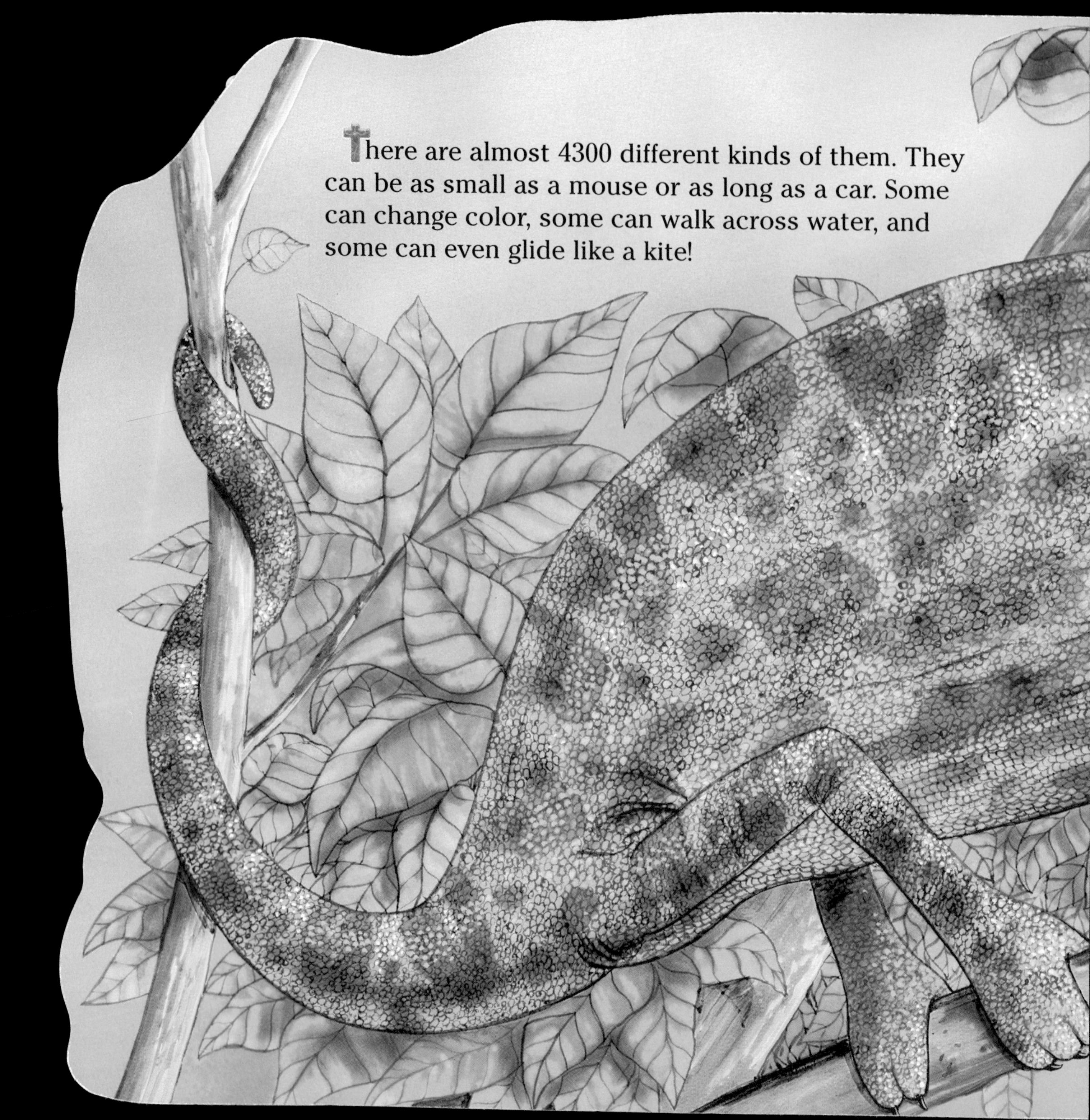

There are almost 4300 different kinds of them. They can be as small as a mouse or as long as a car. Some can change color, some can walk across water, and some can even glide like a kite!

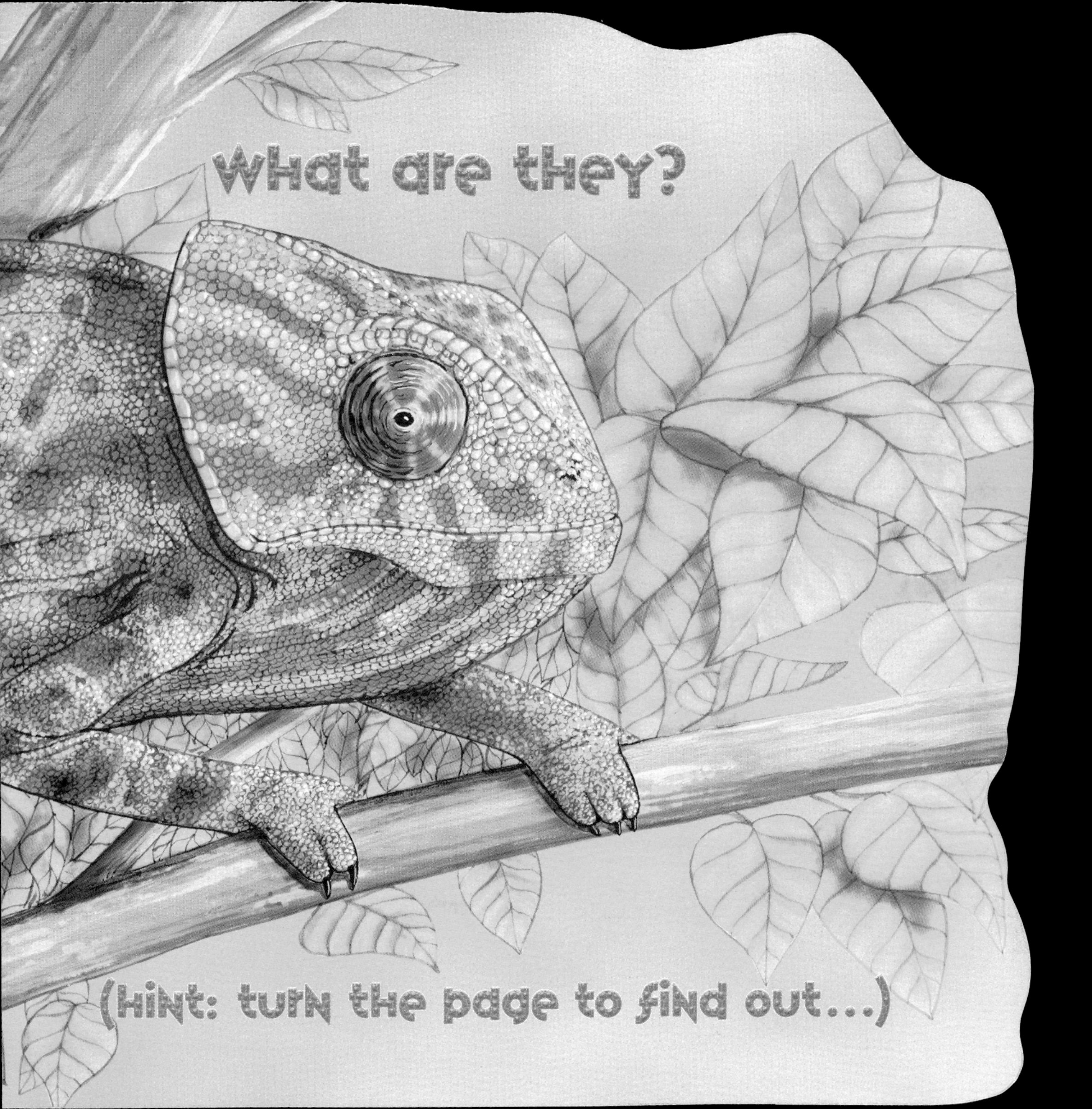
What are they?
(hint: turn the page to find out...)

# What is a lizard?

It's a kind of animal called a **reptile**. All reptiles are cold-blooded, which means that the temperature of their bodies is the same as the temperature of the air around them. To keep warm, a lizard often lies in the sun. But to cool down, it hides in the shade.

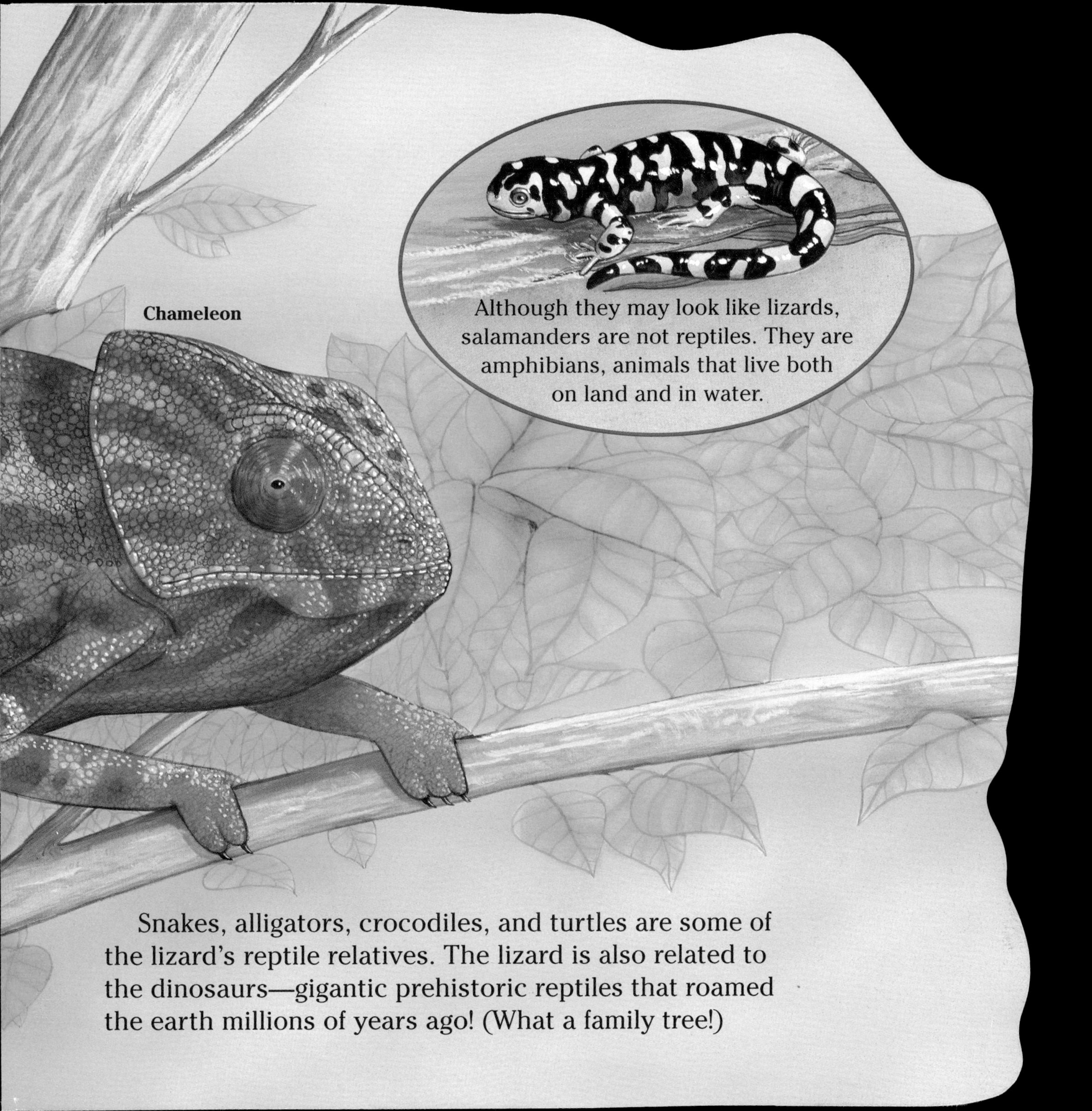


Although they may look like lizards, salamanders are not reptiles. They are amphibians, animals that live both on land and in water.

Snakes, alligators, crocodiles, and turtles are some of the lizard's reptile relatives. The lizard is also related to the dinosaurs—gigantic prehistoric reptiles that roamed the earth millions of years ago! (What a family tree!)

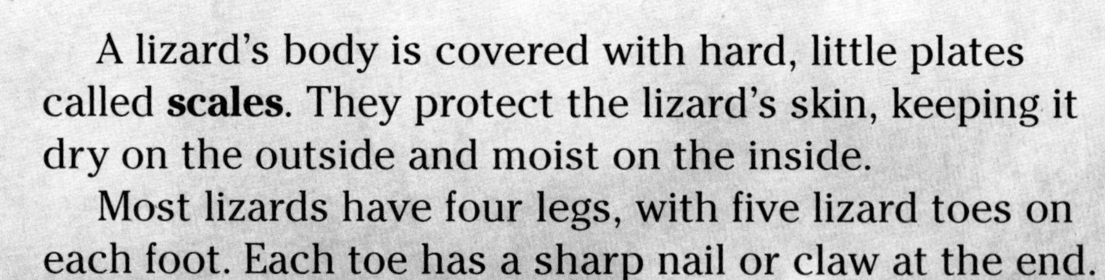

A lizard's body is covered with hard, little plates called **scales**. They protect the lizard's skin, keeping it dry on the outside and moist on the inside.

Most lizards have four legs, with five lizard toes on each foot. Each toe has a sharp nail or claw at the end. Lizards use their claws to climb and to fight. (Better trim those, buddy!)

Lizards also have long tails. Some can use their tails to help them climb and grip things. Others use their tails like a whip to defend themselves!

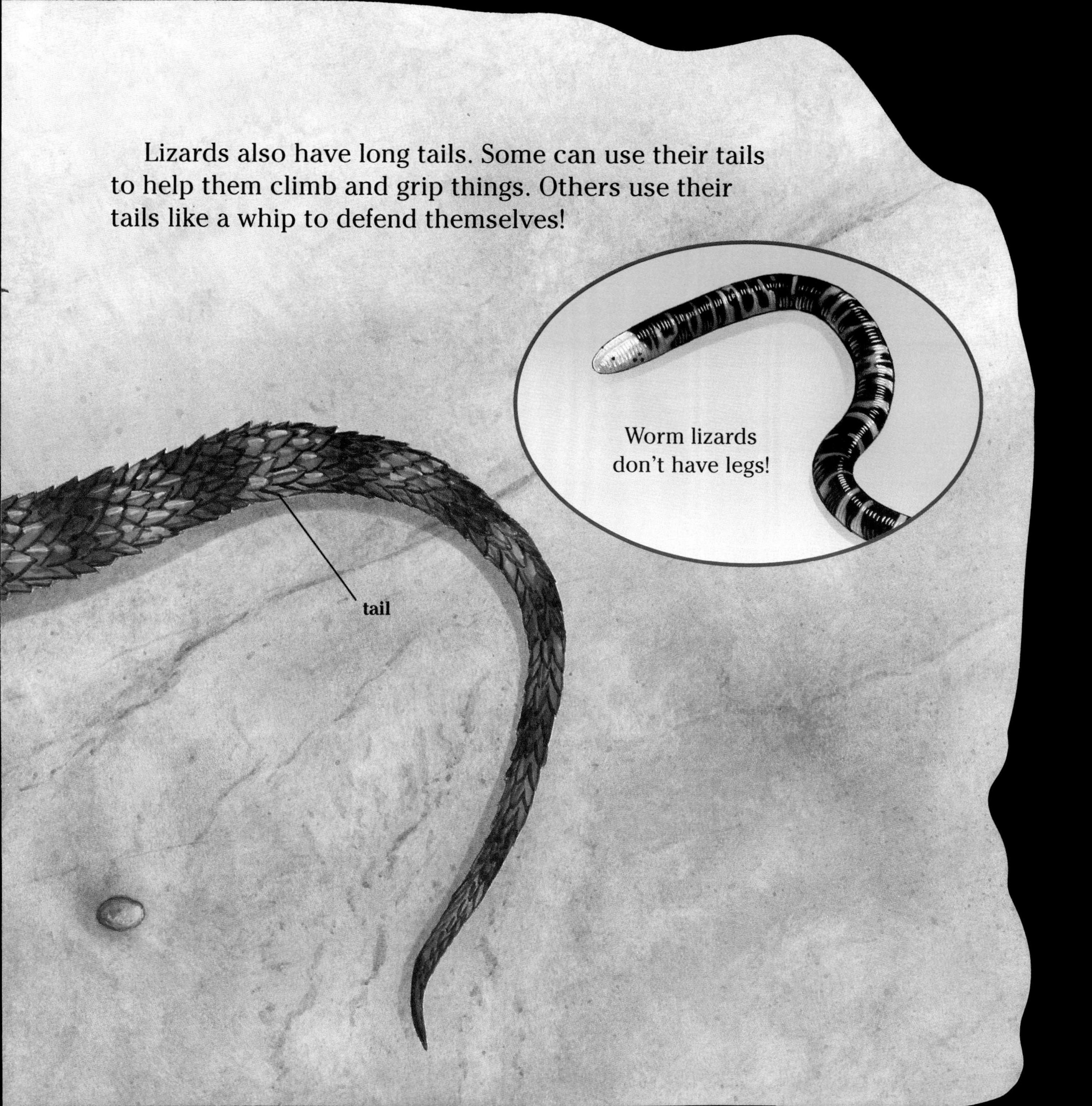

Lizards have two big eyes and can see very well. Some lizards can even look in two directions at the same time! Unlike snakes, lizards have eyelids. And except in a few species, the eyelids can move up and down!

**Tokay gecko**

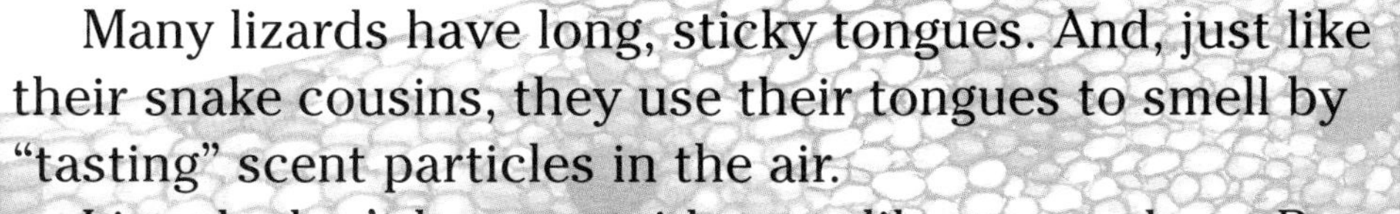

Many lizards have long, sticky tongues. And, just like their snake cousins, they use their tongues to smell by "tasting" scent particles in the air.

Lizards don't have outside ears like you and me. But they can hear through two small ear openings on either side of their head.

## Body Parts

**Most lizards have:**

- Scales
- Four legs, five toes on each foot
- A long tail
- 2 eyes with eyelids
- A long tongue
- Ear openings

# Where do lizards live?

All over the world—in fact, they can be found on every continent except icy Antarctica. Lizards HATE the cold, so they usually hang out where the climate is hot—in blistering deserts, steamy rain forests, sunny mountains, and warm plains.

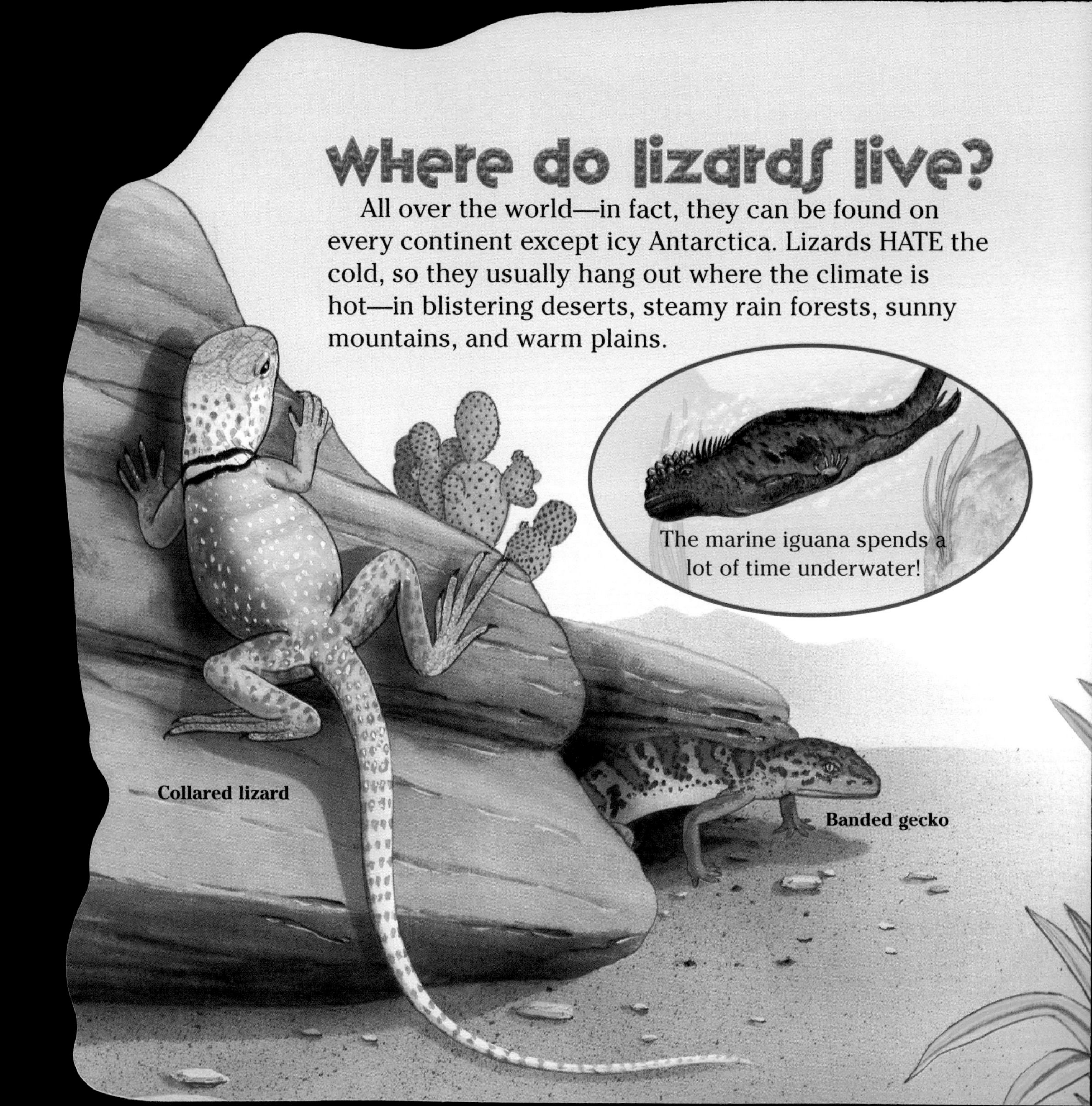


The marine iguana spends a lot of time underwater!

Lizards make their homes on the ground, in the trees, or in underground burrows. Some even like to live in people's houses. Lizards are everywhere!

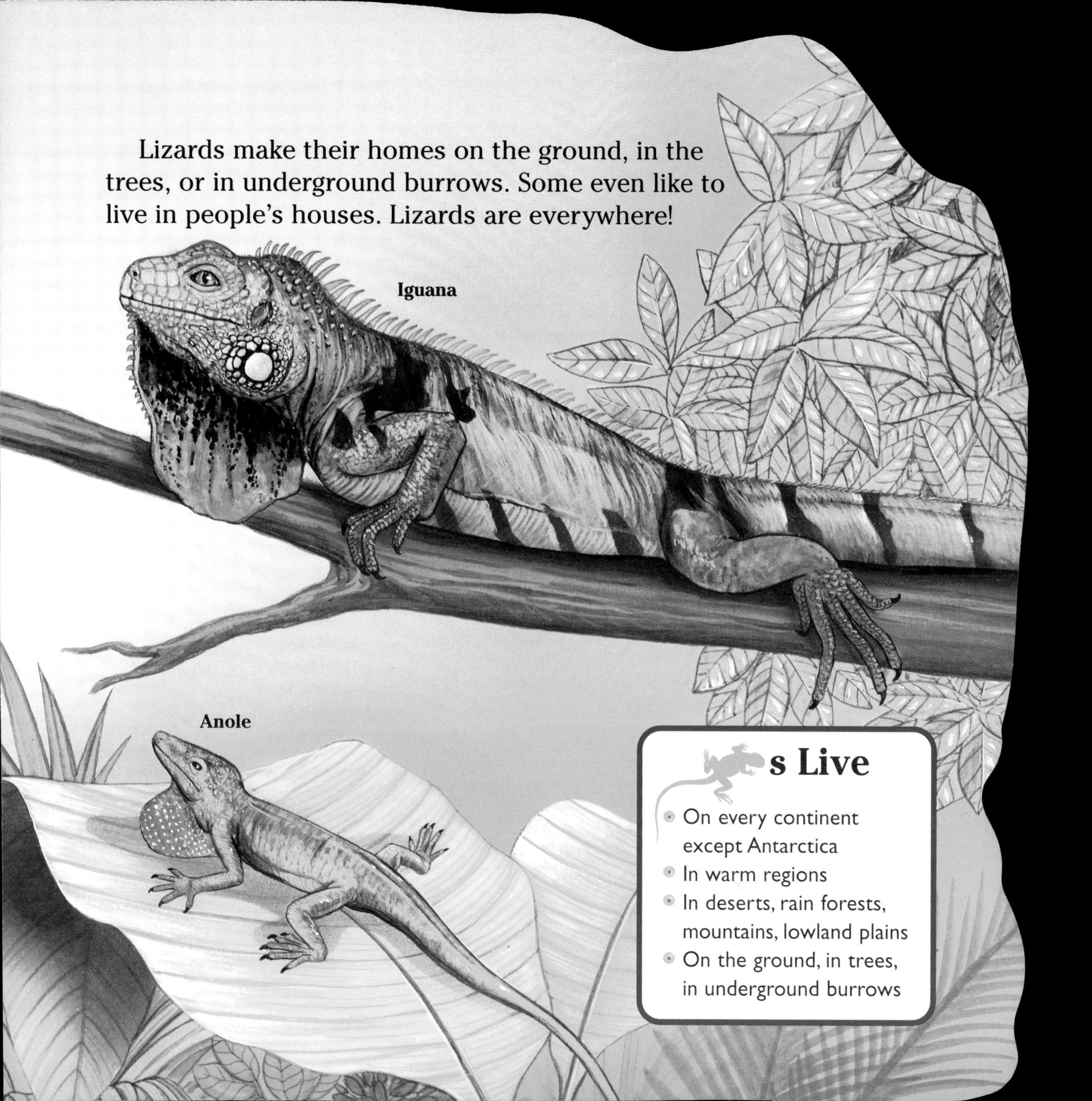


## s Live

- On every continent except Antarctica
- In warm regions
- In deserts, rain forests, mountains, lowland plains
- On the ground, in trees, in underground burrows

# What do lizards eat?

Mostly insects and small animals—ants, flies, centipedes, spiders, scorpions, worms, grubs, snails, and slugs. (Yum!) Some lizards are large enough to eat mice, birds, and even other lizards. A few lizards eat plants, vegetables, and fruits.

Gila monster

The chameleon lashes out its long, sticky tongue like a lasso—then reels an unsuspecting bug into its mouth!

The largest lizard of all, the Komodo dragon, is big enough to kill and eat wild pigs, goats, and even deer. Better not get too close—or it might try to eat YOU!

Young Komodo dragons have to hide up in trees. Otherwise, they will become an adult Komodo dragon's lunch!

## s Eat

- Ants, flies, centipedes, spiders, scorpions
- Worms, grubs, snails, slugs
- Plants, vegetables, fruit
- Larger lizards eat mice, birds, and other lizards.
- Komodo dragons eat wild pigs, sheep, and deer.

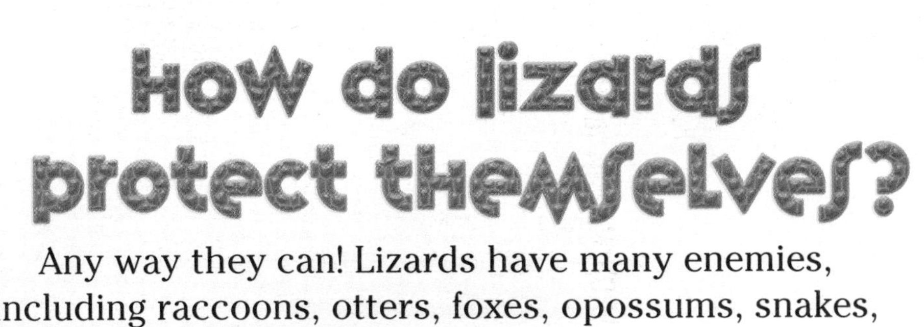

# How do lizards protect themselves?

Any way they can! Lizards have many enemies, including raccoons, otters, foxes, opossums, snakes, hawks, badgers, and other lizards. So they have many different ways of defending themselves.

Most lizards just run and hide, or play dead. Some have sharp horns and spines. Others flash brightly colored body parts or hiss loudly to keep enemies away.

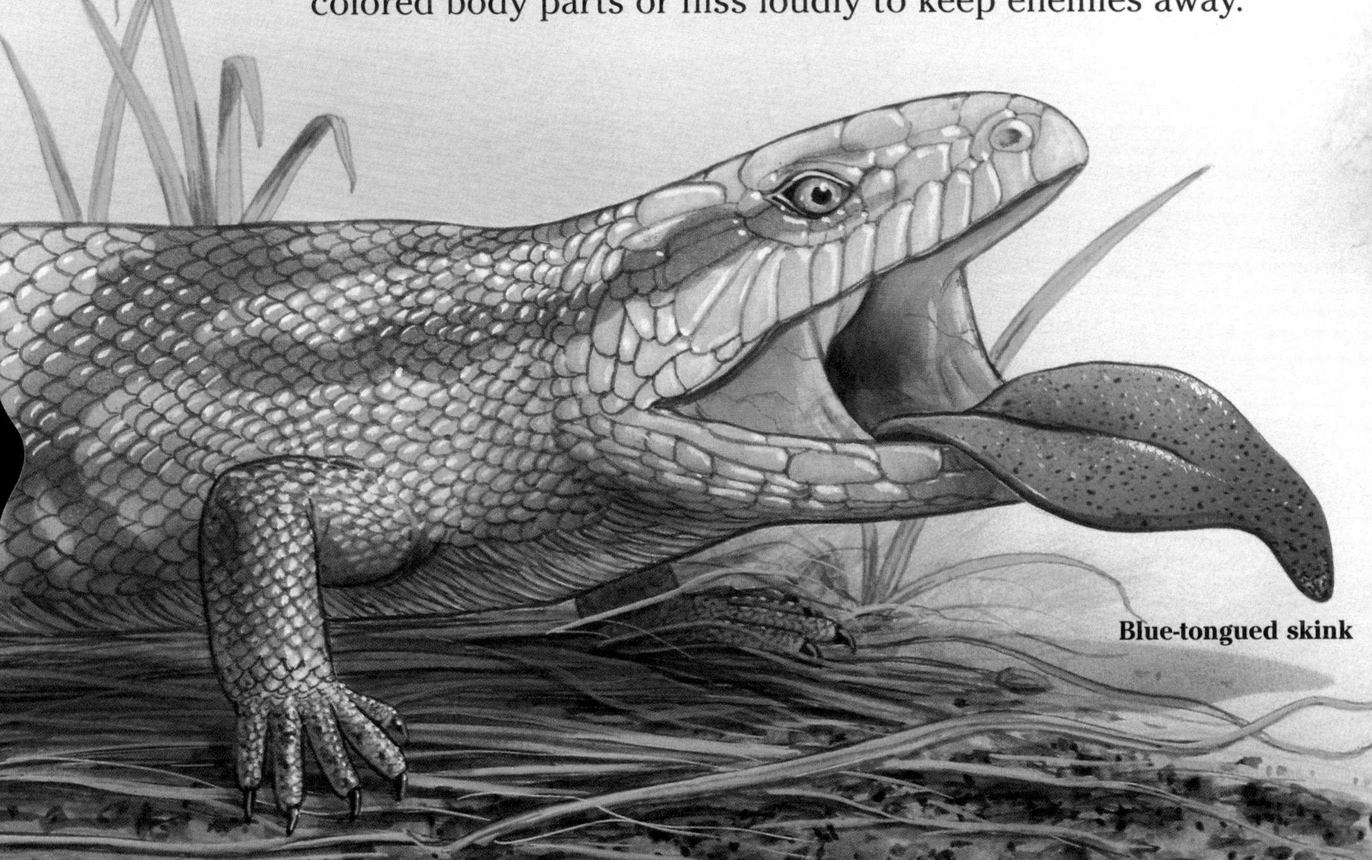

**Blue-tongued skink**

Believe it or not, many lizards can actually break off their own tail if attacked. The tail will continue to move, and hopefully distract a hungry animal long enough for a getaway. (Don't worry! The tail grows back in a few weeks.)

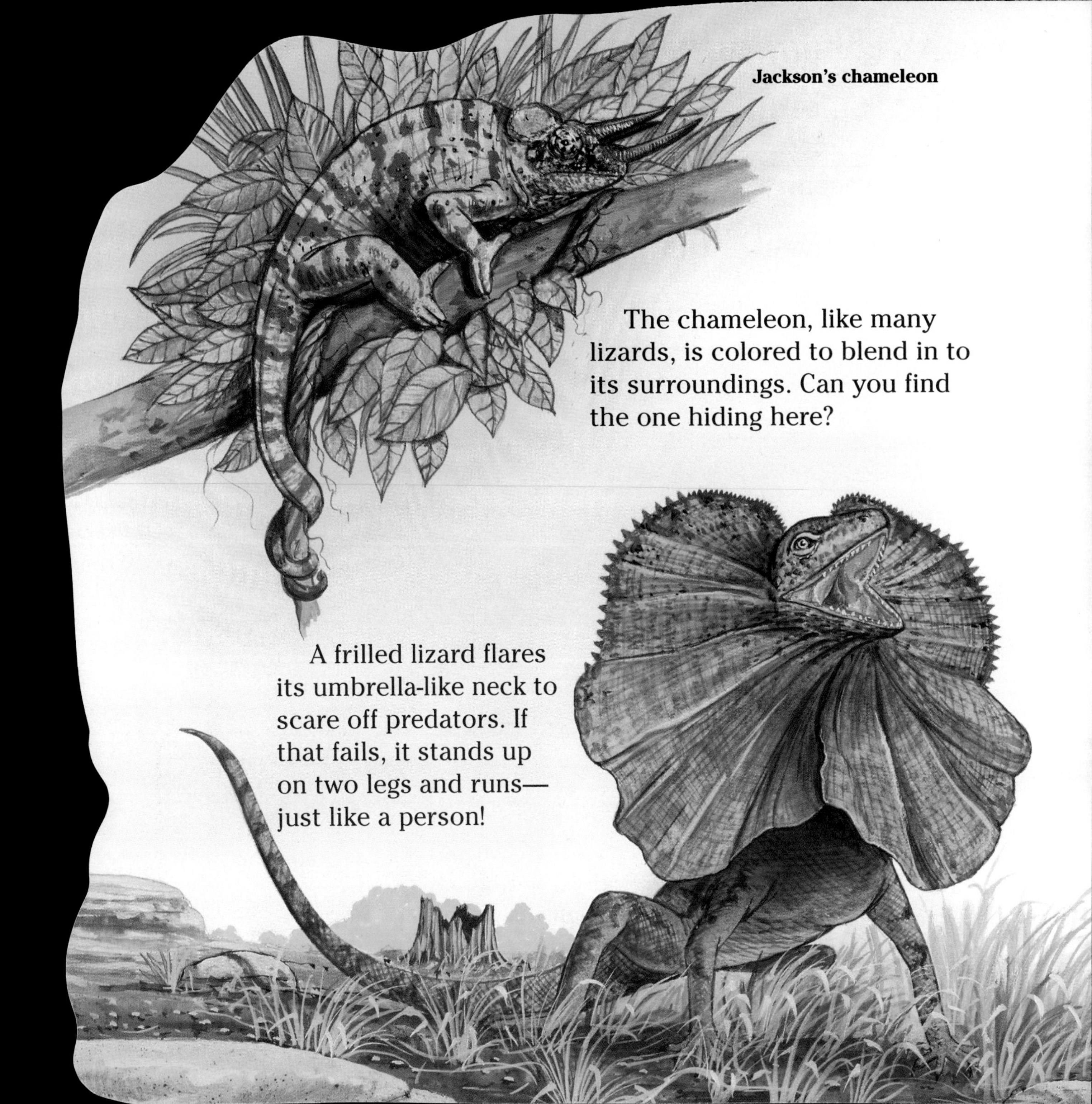

**Jackson's chameleon**

The chameleon, like many lizards, is colored to blend in to its surroundings. Can you find the one hiding here?

A frilled lizard flares its umbrella-like neck to scare off predators. If that fails, it stands up on two legs and runs—just like a person!

But why run if you can fly. The flying dragon can glide away from danger. It has large flaps of skin on either side of its belly that it uses like a hang glider!

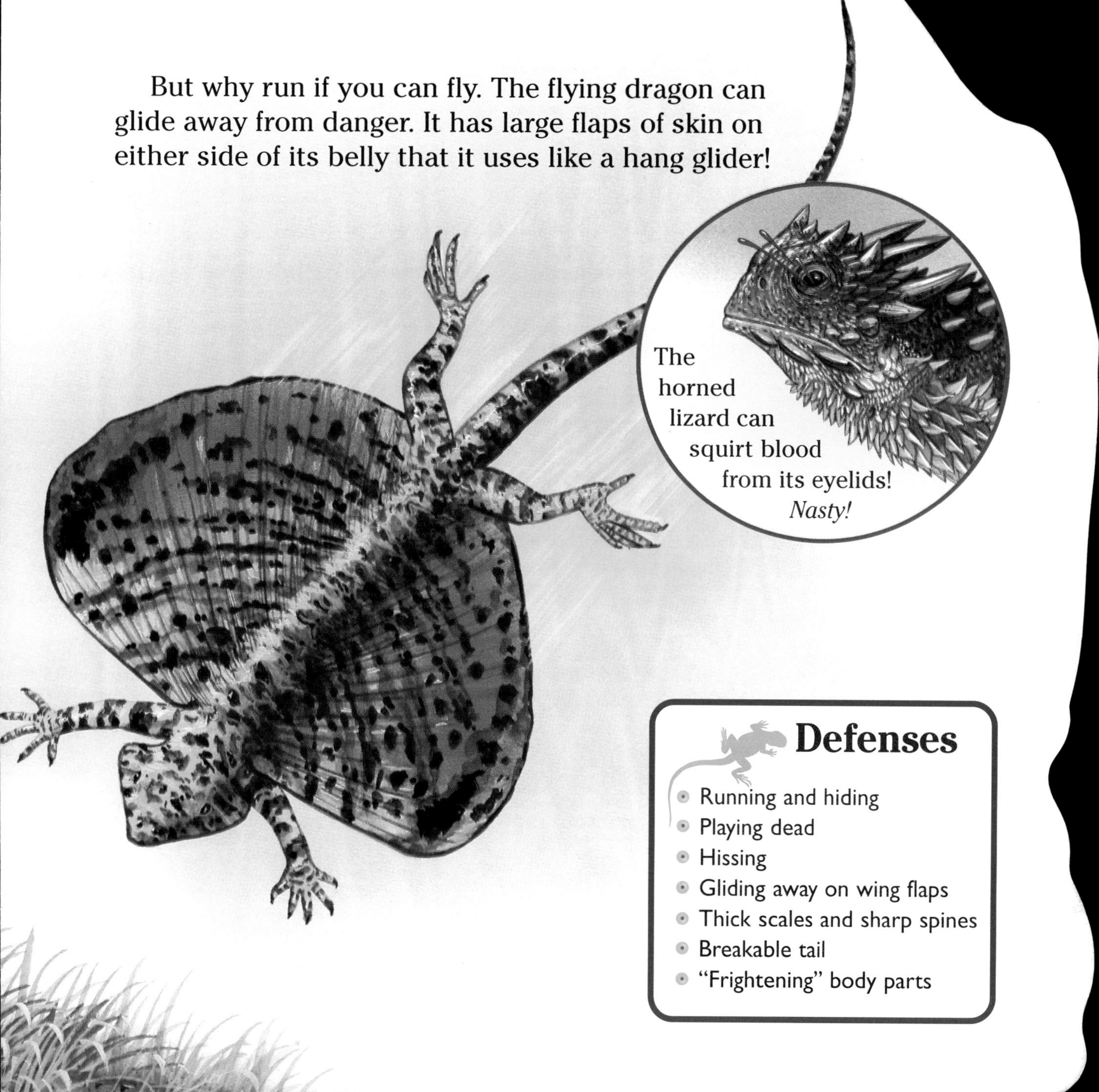

The horned lizard can squirt blood from its eyelids! *Nasty!*

## Defenses

- Running and hiding
- Playing dead
- Hissing
- Gliding away on wing flaps
- Thick scales and sharp spines
- Breakable tail
- "Frightening" body parts

# Where do baby lizards come from?

From mommy lizards, of course! Most female lizards lay eggs—usually between 1 and 25! But a few kinds of females bear live young.

Eggs take from two weeks to a few months to hatch. As soon as a little lizard leaves the shell, it is ready to take care of itself.

Baby lizards have a special egg tooth that they use to break out of their shells.

As lizards grow, they sometimes get too big for their own skin. So they grow a new skin under the old one. When the new skin is ready, the old one flakes off in patches. This is called **molting**.

Iguanas

## Beginnings

- Female usually lays between 1 and 25 eggs.
- In 2 weeks to a few months, the eggs hatch.
- Some lizards bear live young.

# Bet you didn't know...

Gila monsters are venomous! They can easily kill a small animal with one bite.

Some male lizards attract females by puffing up their throats like balloons.

Flying dragons glide up to 195 feet (60 meters) between trees and the ground!

Komodo dragons grow to over 10 feet (3 meters) long and weigh more than 300 pounds (135 kilograms)!

A basilisk can run right across the water's surface!

Now that's just about everything you need to know . . .

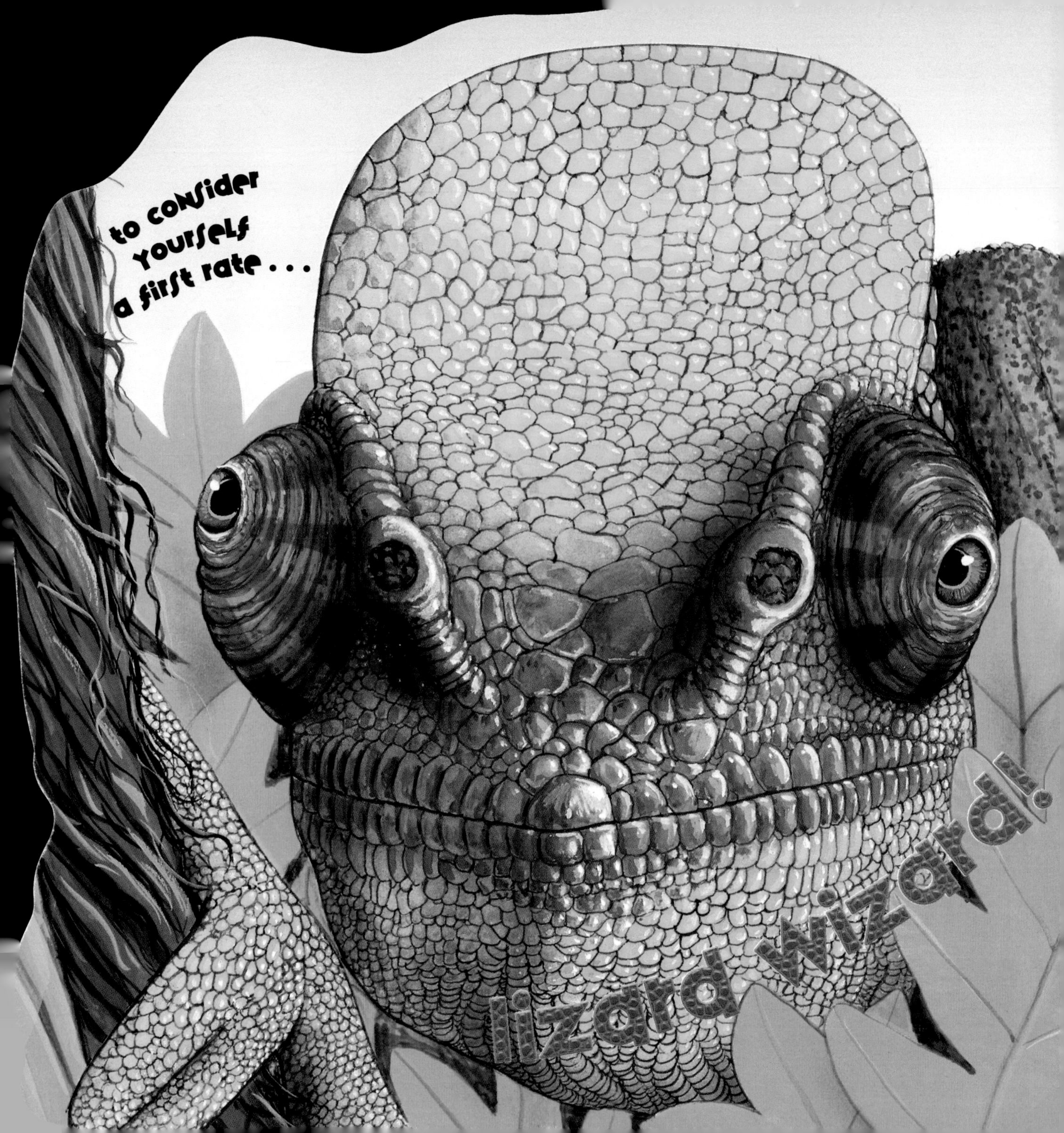
to consider
yourself
a first rate . . .
lizard wizard!